LITTLE CITIZENS

WE ARE HONEST

DWAYNE HICKS

PowerKiDS press.

Published in 2023 by The Rosen Publishing Group, Inc.
2544 Clinton St, Buffalo, NY 14224

First Edition

Editor: Theresa Emminizer
Book Design: Rachel Rising

Photo Credits: Cover, M_Agency/Shutterstock.com; pp. 4, 6, 8, 10, 12, 14, 16, 18, 20 somen/Shutterstock.com; pp. 5, 9 Africa Studio/Shutterstock.com; p. 7 Hananeko_Studio/Shutterstock.com; pp. 11, 13 wavebreakmedia/Shutterstock.com; p. 15 Sergey Novikov/Shutterstock.com; p. 17 Jozefina777/Shutterstock.com; p. 19 Olya Komarova/Shutterstock.com; p. 21 ESB Professional/Shutterstock.com.

Some of the images in this book illustrate individuals who are models. The depictions do not imply actual situations or events.

Library of Congress Cataloging-in-Publication Data

Names: Shea, Therese, author.
Title: We are honest / Therese Shea.
Description: Buffalo, New York : PowerKids Press, [2023] | Series: Little citizens | Includes bibliographical references and index. |
Identifiers: LCCN 2022020900 (print) | LCCN 2022020901 (ebook) | ISBN 9781538389126 (library binding) | ISBN 9781538389102 (paperback) | ISBN 9781538389133 (ebook)
Subjects: LCSH: Honesty–Juvenile literature.
Classification: LCC BJ1533.H7 S525 2023 (print) | LCC BJ1533.H7 (ebook) | DDC 179/.9–dc23/eng/20220630
LC record available at https://lccn.loc.gov/2022020900
LC ebook record available at https://lccn.loc.gov/2022020901

Manufactured in the United States of America

CPSIA Compliance Information: Batch #CWPK23. For Further Information contact Rosen Publishing, New York, New York at 1-800-237-9932.

CONTENTS

A Good Citizen

You belong to a community. You are a member of your country. You are a **citizen**! Citizens have **rights**. We also have **responsibilities**. We need to act a certain way for the good of everyone. Good citizens are honest.

Tell the Truth

Being honest means being truthful. It is not always easy to do that. Sometimes we make mistakes by accident. Sometimes we don't think about the **consequences** of doing something wrong. It can be really hard to **admit** when we are wrong!

Be Brave

Being honest means being brave. We might worry we will get in trouble if we tell the truth. But if we are honest, others will trust us. Being honest might also mean that someone else will not get in trouble for our actions.

Honesty in Action

Lucas was playing in the house with a ball. The ball broke a window. His dad asked who did it. Lucas needs to decide if he will be honest. He could blame it on his brother. He could say he does not know.

Lucas tells his dad he broke the window. His dad tells him he is proud of him for being honest. Lucas did the right thing. Lucas and his dad clean up the mess together. Then they go outside to play ball.

Be Fair

Being honest also means being fair. Honest people play by the rules. They do not try to cheat others. Dishonest people might try to have more of something. They might break rules to win. But that means that others will not trust them.

Honesty in Action

Grace's mom gives her four pieces of candy. She tells Grace to give two pieces to her sister Ivy. Grace eats her two pieces quickly. Grace wonders if she should keep another piece and give Ivy just one piece.

Grace thinks about how Ivy would feel. Grace decides to be honest. She gives Ivy two candy pieces. Grace is honest. It is fair that they each got two pieces. Grace would want Ivy to be honest and fair too!

Honesty Wins!

Honest people are truthful about what they say and what they do. It is not always easy to be honest! But others trust honest people. They want to play games with them. They want to be friends with them. Honest people make good friends!

GLOSSARY

admit: To make known, often unwillingly, that you did something.

citizen: One who lives in a country legally and has certain rights.

consequence: What happens as the result of an action.

responsibility: Something a person is in charge of.

right: Something someone is allowed to have, get, or do by law.

FOR MORE INFORMATION

BOOKS

Nelson, Penelope. *Being Fair*. Minneapolis, MN: Jump!, Inc., 2020.

Santos, Rita. *Zoom In on Honesty.* New York, NY: Enslow Publishing, 2019.

WEBSITES

Honesty
ny.pbslearningmedia.org/resource/aim17-sel-honestycomic/arthur-honesty-francines-tough-day/
Read about honesty in an interactive comic.

Small Talk—Honesty—CBC Kids
www.youtube.com/watch?v=KvzgvaTnqek
Watch young people talk about honesty in this video.

INDEX